Mult-I-Tasking

The Brief Guide
For
Your Busy Life

Dr. William Gordon, CEC/ACC

Revolutionary Imprints
Chicago, IL
2007

Revolutionary Imprints is a
Division of
Capax Coaching, Ltd.
5417 N. Ashland Ave.
Chicago, IL 60640
312.479.6301

ISBN: 978-0-6151-7387-0

If you enjoy this volume, consider trainings on e-mail effectiveness and time management that can be customized to meet your individual needs. Please contact the author for additional information regarding trainings and seminars, keynotes, and workshops on these and other topics.

See our website at www.capaxcoaching.com

.

Getting direction in life is only relevant if you have some idea where you wish to go and where you have been. Ultimately, you really need to know where you are. Figuring that out may be far more difficult than the journey itself.

Table of Contents

Introduction

It is common in the opening pages of books for the author to prepare the reader for what is to come next, explain his or her particular viewpoint, and share some insights into why this book was written. This could make for a very brief introduction.

Very simply stated, this book addresses some of the biggest consumers. By that, I don't mean to suggest that this book will sell millions of copies to hungry consumers who want to make certain that they have procured this thrilling volume. When I speak of consumers here, what I am really intending to address are those elements of our lives that consume us most, those being issues of time management and e-mail. And equally simply, what is to come in this book is the shocking reality that if you don't do something about these two issues, they will quickly become out of control and consume you, just as they do countless others.

An introduction addresses the author's motivation, and often specifies for whom the book is written. That is even the shortest answer yet. It is written for people like me and people like you. How would I know that it is written for someone like you? Because if you are reading these words, I am pretty certain that either you have an interest in knowing more about these topics, or someone around you who gave you the book to read thinks you should have an interest in them. In other words, pay attention.

The format of this book is about as simple as everything else. I have written as few paragraphs as I gracefully could get away with and still fully explain myself. The vast majority of this information is shared in bullet points. Who has time for anything else these days? This book is not likely to be a book you will pick up and read excitedly from beginning to end. It is a book, however, that lends itself to the practices it promotes:

- It is small. It will fit easily into a pocket, briefcase, purse, man-bag, airline seat pocket, or wherever else you slide things you are reading in between other major events in your life.

- It is categorized by topics for easy reference.
- It is in larger print so you don't have to find your reading glasses.

In researching this book, I have been amused a number of times with how much authors of time-management books and articles eloquently and verbosely explain themselves, carrying on chapter after chapter about efficiency. One such tome even advised the reader to "set a goal to buy a planner" rather than simply starting the process outright.

- If you are unable to manage yourself enough to set a goal to buy a planner without reading several chapters inviting you to consider the possibility of planning in the first place, this book isn't for you. Such practices are known pretty commonly for their quality of "F.T.I." This is when you spend so much time planning for action that you "fail to implement".
- If you are ready to plunge in, you may have picked up the right volume. This book is likely to be one you will simply thumb through from time to time to pick

up an idea or two to try in your own life. Most of them are relatively simple and some of them will fit you and your lifestyle well. Others won't be for you. Ignore those, and find one that works.

- Don't be afraid to try ideas that fail for you. Just because I haven't presented an idea or perhaps explained it in a way that will allow you to be successful, don't fret. It doesn't mean the idea is bad, or that you are somehow a miserable, cosmic time-management failure. Some of the ideas presented will work well for the vast majority of folks who are left-brain dominant, and some will work better for those who are more likely to be creative. But whatever you do, try something. The worst killer of efficiency and effectiveness is the belief that you cannot change.

- Practice with it for a while before you decide you can't do it or it doesn't work well for you. In the end, you will find something that meets the needs you had when you picked the book up in the first place.

With all of that said, one final word about the book and about my perspective as an author. Notice the title of the book? It has a capital letter "I" in the middle of the title. Normally, you wouldn't find the word multitasking broken out that way. Hopefully, you get the point that Stephen Covey (a giant in the field of time management) made when he wrote, "(T) he challenge is not to manage time, but to manage ourselves." These issues are predators, ready to eat up your life, your time, your happiness, and your success. They are, however, truly paper tigers... and can be more easily managed than you may have previously believed. But the "I" that represents who you are is going to have to stand up and make some changes.

With all of that said, here is the end of the introduction, less than one thousand words later. I had hoped to be more succinct. Nonetheless, here is the most direct, straightforward book on the market about how to manage yourself around the busy issues of your life.

WEG

Time Management

Time management is a topic too often reserved for business discussions, sorely missing the mark in terms of personal and individual organizational issues. Unfortunately, too many models are built on the early efforts of time management that were geared only toward repetitive tasks (such as manufacturing) or were task-oriented. The latter efforts spoke to managers, but have little to do with what is really demanded of those who supervise others in today's business climate: leadership.

One estimate suggests that if you spend a minute of planning time for tasks that are related to repetitive motions, you can increase efficiency by approximately a 1:3 ratio. For every minute you spend planning, you can save three minutes in accomplishing the task. While not a bad investment in and of itself, those same estimates say that if the task being planned for is related to issues other than repetitive motion, such as from the neck up, the ratio increases to 1:10. Ten minutes are saved for every minute of planning.

Whether or not you choose to believe those numbers are true, two things ought to quickly jump out at us. The first is that planning pays. The second is that it may not take all that much to save time. Ah, but ten minutes? I can hear the skeptics furrowing their rigid brows now. Ten minutes doesn't sound like a lot until I add today's ten minutes to tomorrow's. By the end of the week, I have saved fifty minutes. Even if I take four weeks of vacation a year where I suspend my planning efforts and squander those ten minutes, it still figures out to 2400 minutes a year—the equivalent of one full week of work. Or pleasure, depending on how you choose to spend your saved time!

Following are some time saving techniques that are intended to serve two purposes. The first is to make you more efficient. That is nice. But more importantly, I hope they make you more effective. In my book, effective trumps efficient every time. Let me give you a wild example. Suppose that I am working in Boston and want to return to my home in Chicago. Most of us learned in public school mathematics that the most efficient route (the shortest) between two points is a straight line. If I choose efficiency over effectiveness, I might then point my car exactly at Chicago as I sit in Copley Square in downtown Boston, and start driving a straight line. Is it efficient? Well, because it is not at all effective to drive where there are no roads, running through buildings, cutting across traffic, trying to negotiate bodies of water without bridges, and so forth, it proves not to be truly efficient, as well. What I really want is to get to Chicago, and in this case the shortest route doesn't really get me to what I want.

In time management issues, the same may hold true. Let's say, for instance, that one of the strategies outlined in this section works well for thousands of other people, increasing their efficiency one-thousand fold whenever they use it, but for whatever reason doesn't work at all for you. You struggle to learn it, but something prevents the tactic from being effective. Even if it is efficient, it is useless to you. The key to this work is to filter out those strategies that work well, that you can implement, and that produce the results you seek. Theory isn't of any value unless you can apply it to your own business or personal situation.

In the end, time management becomes an issue of *personal management.* You will need to filter everything here through your understanding of your values, your circumstances, and how uncomfortable you are in whatever it is that you are presently doing. Uncomfortable? Certainly. If you aren't uncomfortable, you won't change. The chances are that you have already experienced some level of discomfort already, and that is why you are thumbing through this book. Without discomfort, we will lack the motivation to try anything new.

Every morning when you awaken, it is as if there is an empty drinking glass waiting for you on your nightstand. You are compelled to pick it up as you rise from your bed, and the glass will be with you all day. As soon as you come to consciousness, there is someone out there with a pitcher of water, waiting to fill your glass. Maybe it is your family obligation to get out of bed, your need to get to work, or nature is calling you to rise. But whatever it is, you are already on a schedule and have tasks to do. Someone is beginning to put water in the glass. Throughout the day, people approach you with their own pitchers of water and start pouring into your glass. "Got a minute?" "Can I talk to you for a second?" "Will you do me a favor?" Hear that water pouring? The challenge for you is to drink fast enough to keep that water from overflowing the brim and spilling all over. Demands often exceed capacity. Working as hard as you might, others still may get ahead of you, causing your personal glass to overflow. That's stressful. And it isn't that anyone is trying to do it to you, it's that they have needs in their interactions with you, and that metaphorically looks like water pouring. Don't forget, you are also carrying a pitcher, and you keep pouring water in their glasses, as well. And occasionally, you pour into your own glass, hearing words in your head like "should" and "ought to." How to do you get this to stop?

- The first time management strategy is to practice saying (and eventually say others) the word, "No." Learn to set boundaries about what you can and cannot do, and stick with them. No.

Two letters, which if invested properly, will provide you a lot of extra time in your day.

- Learn to eat the proverbial frog. Mark Twain is credited with saying that if you eat a frog first thing in the morning, nothing else worse happens to you during the day. Brian Tracy, a popular author in the field of time management, says that if you have to choose between two frogs to eat, eat the more ugly one first. In other words, do the difficult tasks first thing, and get them done. Imagine how that will affect your energy and imagine how much more you can accomplish during a day if you aren't thinking about all those things you don't want to do!

- If you think about something, write it down. Much of the lost information that causes confusion in our schedules, causing us to miss appointments or deadlines, could be easily avoided by our carrying a small notebook or 3 x 5 card in our pocket and writing things down as we think of them.

- Use the Master List Technique. This technique simply calls for you to take a blank piece of paper (or a new document on a word processor) and spending a few minutes writing down anything that comes to mind. Just like we empty out the memory cards on our digital cameras to make room for whatever is coming, so must we periodically empty our memories. It is similar to the idea of drinking or pouring some out of the glass of water I described earlier. This technique can be done for a time-limited period, or you can do it until you can think of nothing else. In the end, the information captured can be divided into two major categories. One is information, and the other is task. Move the informational items to their appropriate homes in calendars, date books, cell phones, address or contact lists, etc. The tasks now stand out as our *to-do* list. All that is left is for us to prioritize them.

- If you don't have one, get yourself a good organizer or planner. Keep in mind that the best ones are easily accessible and can be easily used.

I don't have strong feelings about paper versus electronic, except that I do know that if you lose your paper organizer, there usually is no back-up for it. Once it is gone, it is gone. Connecting my electronic organizer to my computer means that they both carry the same information. If one goes, I have a system in place to retrieve the lost information.

- Those who want to continue using paper organizers should seriously consider writing in pencil rather than pen. I have seen too many paper organizer systems that are filled with scratch outs, arrows, asterisks, and highlighter marks to try to get them to make sense. When you use pencil, you can also use that remarkable tool called an eraser to make changes without having to figure out your encryptions.

- There are multiple tools for working out your priorities. The simplest I have seen simply asks you to list all of the items in your to-do list. You then consider item number one to item number two and put a check next to the one that is the most important, or first priority. Now compare item one to item three, voting for the most important again. Eventually, you have compared item one to every other item in the list. Now begin with item two, and compare it only those items down the list, checking next to the one that is more important to you. Don't forget you have already compared it to the first item, so you only work *down* the list. Once you have completed those comparisons, start with three, and again work only down the list, and so forth until you get to the last item. In the end, all you are doing is counting the check marks, which are essentially *votes* for the most important item. The one with the most check marks is the most important, and should be done first. The second item with the most votes is priority two, and so on. Simple and effective.

- You may also want to look at quadrant prioritizing, which I believe was first suggested by Dr. Stephen Covey. Begin by creating two intersecting axis lines. The vertical line is marked at the top with the word *urgent* and the bottom of that axis is marked *not urgent*. On the horizontal axis, the left hand side is marked *important*, and the right hand side is marked *not important*. This creates a grid of four panes in which we look at the intersections of the concepts of importance/non-importance, and urgent/non-urgency. First priorities are those items that are both important and urgent. Second, we consider those items that are important, but not urgent. Third, we list those that are not important to us, but may be important to others, and the last quadrant contains items that are neither important nor urgent. His model is also very simple and quite effective for sorting your task lists. I highly recommend it. Urgent is very simply those things that need to be done now, or have an immediately impending deadline. Keep in mind that others may come to you to tell you that something must be done immediately. You will need to decide whether or not you are willing to accept their sense of urgency. Important items are those that are directly related to your pursuit of your own goals. In other words, tasks that aren't going to help you achieve your mission aren't important, even if someone else seems to think they are.

- When planning your schedule, the temptation is going to be to put appointments back-to-back, leaving no space in between them. Unfortunately in our lives, the unplanned and unexpected happens, and so it becomes important to leave room for those events in our schedule. One rule is to always plan about fifty percent more time than you initially believe a task will take you. That means you will have time for the crises and the unexpected.

- Keep a list from your tasks identified in the Master List Technique of items that may take only a few minutes to complete. I refer to this as my five-and-ten list (named after the old five-and-ten cent stores.) These are items that I know need to be completed, but can be safely tucked into my schedule in those found moments, the unused increments of time when a project has gone better than I anticipated.

- Always keep track of the items that you have accomplished in the course of a day. Nothing stresses us more than to perceive that we have worked all day and accomplished nothing. By marking finished tasks on our to-do list, we can review at the end of the day and celebrate our work. I suggest you simply line these items through with a single line, or check them off. Don't mark them out with scratches that obliterate them. If you save your lists of accomplished tasks, you will then also have an historical record of when you did your work, which might be handy later when you get asked about them.

- Don't be afraid to ask other people for help. Sometimes people are pleased that we have included them in a project, as it expands their opportunities or knowledge. For instance, young children can be enrolled in household tasks if we frame them as an opportunity to act like an adult, or do to things normally reserved for older children. Similarly, in our jobs, people may look upon our work or project as an opportunity to expand, and may willingly help. But you won't know that if you don't ask them to first!

- Be very cautious not to get caught in the practice of doing things that are trivia or irrelevant. Occupying ourselves in these tasks allows us to *feel busy* without really being productive. The goal is effective and productive, not the illusion of busyness. Ask yourself several times each day, "Why am I doing what I am doing right now?" and "How is what I am doing moving me toward my life goals?" The answers to those two questions may really surprise you—and reveal that what you are really doing is procrastinating on projects that really do need your attention.

- Use technology or other time savers whenever possible. For instance, I recently purchased on of those small robotic, automatic vacuum cleaners. I have been very pleasantly surprised at how well it works. I can be vacuuming the floor simultaneously with clearing the countertops. We have become accustomed to dishwashers and automatic washers and dryers for our laundry. There are similar new time savers that you might consider.

- Use the telephone and instant messaging where possible. Instant messaging generally consists of short messages, making for efficient communication that keeps us from getting caught in longer conversations that take time. Similarly, using the telephone (including well formed voicemail messages) may save us from emails or letters. Written words are so easily misunderstood because they leave the vocal and visual parts of messages, and rely therefore only on our verbal choices. How many ways can you restate something as simple as "That's not what I said"? The reality is that you can take that to mean several different messages based on the emphasis you put on each word. A quick phone call could resolve the issue.

- Be sure to clear off your desk when you are beginning work. Your brain is easily confused by distractions such as piles of paper on your desk. It can't tell whether you plan to work on those or not, so every time your roving eye catches sight of the piles, the brain begins to think about them. This is called *desk stress*, and can be eliminated by removing piles and other forms of distractions from the desk surface. Move unused items, including pictures of family and friends, from your line of sight, moving them off to the side. In similar fashion, take down all those sticky notes that you have placed around the perimeter of your computer monitor. They play the same tricks on the eyes and brain. How much time might you save? It is estimated that the process of looking up at another project while you are working can cost you as much as 30% in productivity! You don't have to put the beach stone or the character figure from your last vacation away. Just move those things out of your immediate line of sight.

- Block similar activities together. For instance, don't go to the file drawer immediately every time you have a paper that needs to be filed. Create a folder for items that need to be filed. Use a folder instead of a box because they have limited capacity (boxes allow you to pile higher and higher.) Before you go home each night, be sure to do the filing for the day. (See the section on telephone interruptions for this same principle.)

- Use tickler files to remind you of up-coming events such as important work deadlines, birthdays or anniversaries, or a bill that is due. A tickler is simply a reminder planted several days or weeks ahead of a significant event to remind of the upcoming deadline. You might, for instance, file your monthly bills by their due date, but in filing them move them up a full week before the actual date the bill is due. This will allow you to make the payment in time for it to arrive at its destination without costing you an overdue penalty and resulting finance charges. Similarly, by reminding yourself of upcoming personal events, you don't end up sending cards late, or worse yet, showing up to celebrate that event empty handed. Tickle yourself to greater success!

Without question, the simplest and most effective time management technique I can suggest to you is that you plan your work and then work your plan. The vast majority of wasted time is found in our mental fumbling about what to do next and how to get started (procrastination). Working out a plan and working from that plan will make your transitions smoother, and will mean by the end of the day you will more likely have accomplished what you want to get down. Write the plan down. Apparently that imprints our plan differently on our brain, and dramatically increases the likelihood we will achieve our goals. It has been said that those who fail to plan inevitably have a plan to fail. Don't let that be you.

Telephone Calls

T here is a certain disturbing urgency to the sound of a ringing telephone. It really doesn't have to be our home phone ringing in the middle of the night (although that can be very disturbing) to make us want to rush and answer. With the advent of cellular telephones, the phenomenon of ringing telephones has extended beyond our homes and offices, and now seems to be everywhere we are—in our cars, in stores, walking down the streets. We are walking communications centers, and it is nearly impossible to escape the urgency of wanting to answer when we hear the ringing (or more correctly, the ring tone, in whatever format it takes.)

That being said, managing telephone interruptions in our day becomes an especially necessary and difficult task. The more telephones have been made accessible to us, the more we have expected one another to be immediately accessible by telephone.

- Screen calls whenever possible by using caller ID. Simply because someone you know is on the other end of the line doesn't mean you must answer at that moment, particularly if it isn't a good time for you (such as driving a car, or about to receive root canal.)

- Let calls go to voicemail so that you can answer them in groups, at your convenience.

- Change your voicemail to reflect your day, and announce to callers when you will be available to call them back. Generally, callers will be satisfied if you say you will call them back at a particular time as long as you do so. Make certain that you give a time range, such as "between four and five o'clock today" so that you can fit all of your calls in during that time.

- When calling to leave messages for others, be certain to give them several choices of times that they can expect to get you if they call back so that you can end the game of *telephone tag*.

- There are times when it is appropriate to call to create an appointment for a longer telephone call. This gives both parties the opportunity to prepare for the topic of the longer call, and assures that both parties will make themselves available at that time.

- Be clear if you have limited time at the beginning of the telephone call. If someone asks, "Do you have a minute?" and that is what you have, tell them so. That gets them to the point more quickly, and allows you to exit the call when you truly need to without sounding as if you are trying to get out of answering a question or discussing a topic.

- When you need to exit a call, summarize what you have heard. That signals that you are preparing to let the caller go.

- When someone calls you and you are busy, try simply asking him or her, "How can I help you?" This tells them that you are interested in getting to the point of the call without the rude question, "What do you want?"

- Do not take telephone calls when you are in the midst of a conversation with someone else unless you have warned them at the beginning of the chat that you plan to do so. The behavior is simply rude. Similarly, do not ask one person to remain on hold while you speak to another caller unless the first person is waiting to hear information from the second call. It is better to simply plan to call the first caller back later.

- Use conference calling whenever it is necessary to have more than one opinion on the line. This can be especially useful in scheduling or when you simultaneously want to transfer information to both parties. Many cellular services offer this service for free.

- Be careful not to make extended conversations on someone else's cellular time without checking with them first. Often, incoming calls are free. If someone calls you, and you need to extend the conversation with him or her, offer to call back on your nickel.

- When leaving a message on voice mail, always identify yourself fully, tell them what company or department you represent, and leave a return telephone number at the beginning of the message. Speak slowly enough so that they can write. Leave a brief message about the point of your call, and then repeat your name and the contact information again. Many people don't think they need your telephone number until the call is partially through, and then they don't have a pen or pencil handy to write down your contact information. Putting it at the beginning means that when they rewind your message, they don't have to listen to it again to capture the return telephone number.

- Clearly identify who you are at the beginning of conversations even when you are positive the person will recognize your voice. Often our minds are thinking about something else when we answer the telephone, and without the caller clearly identifying who they are, our distractions may make for some awkward moments of trying to get caught back up to the call. Chances are, if you say, "Hi, its me" the person you called may know two or three "me" people in the world. Give their distracted minds a break.

- Under stress, our voices often change pitch, making us much harder to understand. Particularly when we are speaking faster, that can make us very difficult to comprehend. Take a couple of deep breaths before a stressful telephone call, speak slowly and clearly, and pause for the listener to unscramble what you just said.

I suspect most of us would consider telephone communications to be a positive feature of contemporary living. I am personally glad that the television telephones promised to us in the 1960s (where you would see the caller) aren't yet in vogue. There have been many instances where seeing me when you call would perhaps have saved me some time because you would have hung up in horror, but generally speaking, I wouldn't mind a moment's notice before having to show my face in the morning. The power of cellular communications continues to expand, giving even our children the opportunity to be in touch with us on a regular basis. Nonetheless, telephone communications occupy ever-increasing amounts of our days, and like everything else, we need to make conscious choices about how much we want to let them into our lives. For pity sake, don't talk and drive. Even with hands-free sets, the evidence is clear that talking on the telephone makes you more dangerous on the roads; the roads are dangerous enough already. Frankly, I am not convinced that walking on a busy street and talking on your cell phone is a great idea. I have seen too many pedestrians chatter haphazardly crossing against the walk signs at corners, blissfully unaware of the traffic around them. Not only would I not want to be those people, I wouldn't want to be on the other end of the conversation where all you get are the sound effects if something awful does happen. Let's get smarter about telephones.

Planning Your Life

This section ought to be a "read me first", but for many of us, life seems to chug along at its own pace, and we may not believe we have any choices about it at all. While much of the rest of this book is about work or work-related situations, this chapter stands out distinctly with issues that are related to time management in places other than our jobs.

Wouldn't you think that we would have these issues all worked out without bothering to read a book? That would be nice if it were true, but it tends not to be. Following are some simple tips that you can consider to make you life flow more smoothly at home.

- Lay out your clothing the night before. It has been said that it takes us three times longer to select clothing in the morning than it does at night. I suspect this has to do with the stress of our morning schedules, and when we are stressed, we don't make good decisions as quickly. Laying out your clothes the night before also allows you to look for such things as missing buttons, tears, stains, or the need for ironing. When we are hurrying in the morning, those needs tend to make us select something else because we lack the time to address them.

- Consider using technology to your advantage. Rather than running your washer or dryer during the day, try doing it at night as you sleep. Energy demands are lower during that time, and you may actually save money on your energy bill as a result. Use a dishwasher if you have it. In balance, it takes less water than washing the dishes by hand, and it frees you up for other tasks. Also, consider one of those little robotic vacuum cleaners for your home. I use one and find that it does an acceptable job, working merrily away while I engage in other morning tasks. Use you self-cleaning or self-defrosting settings on your major appliances.

- Keep a recording device (such as a micro cassette recorder or a digital recorder) in the car next to you to gather your thoughts or bright ideas that come to you while driving.

- Remove clothing from the dryer as soon as the cycle is done to reduce wrinkling, and thus ironing. Purchase wrinkle-free clothing when you can, but avoid using dryer sheets, as they may corrupt the wrinkle-free coating on your clothing. Wash and dry your wrinkle-frees together if you really want to use dryer sheets for you bedding and towels.

- If you need to iron, do your ironing for the week so that you are setting up the ironing board and heating the iron only once.

- When moving from one room of the house to another, look to see if any misplaced item needs to go along for the ride. That will save you steps when cleaning day comes.

- Create a shopping list that mirrors the order in which items appear in the aisles of your most frequently used market. If you can, standardize the list and copy it so that items that are needed that week can simply be checked off. That way, everyone in the family can help be responsible for the shopping list, ending the need for repeated trips to the store.

- Put a plastic boot tray near your entry door, and have shoes and boots removed there, rather than tracking moisture and dirt throughout your home. The extra benefit is that you will lessen the likelihood of someone misplacing their sneakers just before they are due out the door to catch a bus or train.

- Have a place for everyone in your family to store essential items when they come in the door. Items such as briefcases, backpacks, purses, etc. belong in their proper place, not on the kitchen table when you are trying to prepare dinner.

- Gas up your car anytime you have the time and it is at the half full mark. Don't wait until you are running on vapors. Train new drivers in your family to follow this rule, as well. Invariably, leaving the tank empty will mean you have to stop for gas when you are in the greatest hurry.

- Do your laundry whenever you have a load that needs washing. Don't wait and do the laundry all at once if you have the capacity in your home to do it more frequently. Small quantities are easier to put away in five or ten minutes of folding than is a week's worth (or more), and will provide you greater choices to wear.

- Clean out junk drawers or catch all areas while you are on hold on the telephone.

- Consider getting a headset that can plug into your cordless telephone. It will free up your hands for taking notes, if necessary, or will allow you to attend to other tasks while talking with friends, etc.

- If you watch television, consider getting the technology that allows you to digitally record the programs you watch. If you set the system to record you favorite programs, you can watch them according to your own schedule, and additionally can eliminate any troubling scenes or time-consuming interruptions in your program.

- If you have commercials in your television programming, use these to multitask, such as paying the bills, working on a short project, folding laundry, etc.

- When possible, learn to pay your bills electronically through your on-line banking. This will eliminate addressing and stamping envelopes and scheduling time to drop by the mailbox to get them mailed before a finance charge gets assessed! It is a bit of investment in time to set up the accounts to pay the bills the first time, but you will see your work returned in the ease and speed of this tiresome task in the months that follow.

- Use your driving time to listen to books on CD, especially those that are going to help you in other areas of your life. Chatter radio isn't as likely to educate you as good choices in CDs are. Many libraries have sign-out programs for CDs, just like they do books. Consider using your MP3 player to capture and access these, as well.

- Taking the time to instruct your children in household tasks means that they can succeed in doing them. If you want help around the house, you will need to invest time in your children's education about these tasks.

- If you have tasks or errands that must be run, group them together whenever possible. It takes you less time to run across town once for three tasks than it does to run across town three times. Plan for these, and then work with that plan. Similarly, group family appointments together whenever you can. It takes less time to take several people to a dentist at once than it does to take each on individually.

- Always keep a book, a magazine article, or a CD/MP3 player with you when going for errands appointments. The inevitable wait before going in for your stylist or medical appointment can be used reading and studying things that are helpful to you, rather than whatever happens to be handy.

- Keep shower scum spray and mildew inhibitors in the shower stall for use after the last shower of the day. It is actually easier to clean the stall as you prepare to shower, so consider giving it a good scrubbing before cleaning up yourself. The scum and mildew inhibitors will decrease the number of times you need to be in there scrubbing away. Spray the mildew inhibitors only as you leave the shower. Do not inhale the fumes.

- Use surface wipes to clean counters, sinks, and faucets in your bathroom. They cannot only disinfect, but have shine agents that will make your work very apparent to others!

- Use commercial *cleaning erasers* to clean black marks off the wall. They are quite effective at doing so without removing the paint.

- Clean rooms by working around the face of a clock. Start at one point, and work your way to the right until you return to your starting area. This assures that you get all areas of the room.

Avoid the temptation to go from one room to another carrying items that need to be put away, as you are likely to see something else that needs your attention, and not finish the task at hand. Work where you are, then transport the errant items later.

- Mark books you are reading with a mark on the outside edge to indicate how far you have read. I do this with a highlighter, or I put a pencil mark on those books I do not want to deface. This way, you won't have to worry about bookmarks falling out, particularly as you carry them with you to read in the found moments of your day.

- Everything in the section on time management related to planning and prioritizing applies in this section about your life, as well. There are things you need to be doing in your life that either keep you on track for how you want your life to be, or allow you to move forward on the goals you have set. Plan your life.

Particularly in this section, one must view the suggestions as one does food in a cafeteria. Choose only those that look like they will be good for you. Nobody expects you to consume them all. These sorts of change are better taken in one at a time. Take the ideas and try them out (give them a fair chance to work) and then tweak them to fit you and your lifestyle. In the end, you are likely to find solutions that you can live with and will continue to practice. That is a far better outcome than doing anything simply because you read it in a book.

It has been said that if you can discipline yourself enough to do anything for thirty days, it will become a habit. While I suspect that is true, I also know that if I find something that makes my life easier, I will continue doing it. That's the best kind of habit for me!

Paperwork

Whenever it was that whoever it was invented the Internet (that seems to be the subject of some controversy), the U.S. Government predicted that by the year 2005 we would live in an essentially paperless society. Instead, almost everyone agrees that we have more paper than ever on our desks, and we continue to cut down trees to support our documentation habit!

Why would that be the case? I invite you consider what happens when something important comes across your desk electronically. Since the vast majority of office systems are not equipped with an electronic filing system that moves important documentation to a paperless holding area, we print. When we are open in one application (such as e-mail) and get a date or a telephone that belongs in another system (such as our e-calendar or e-contact list) we print the document to complete the transfer later. Essentially, we either lack the equipment or the expertise to handle our documents electronically, and so we resort to what we do know, which is having paper copies for our files, to retain information for later use. Hence, many of us are buried in piles of paper, and often those pieces of paper are piled up on our desks! That becomes a time management issue as well as a simple organizational one. See the section on time management to see why you need to get these piles off your desk.

- There are a relatively few people who can "file by pile". Those are the folks who have piles of paper in their office, but if you ask them for an invoice from 1997, they can go directly to the pile and pull it out. The rest of us ("Hang on a minute, I know it's in here somewhere...") are fooling ourselves by thinking our piles are really some sort of filing. If you can legitimately file by pile, make certain you have the space to do so off from your working desk. That will likely mean you will need a side table or shelving on which to place the paper. If it is a system that truly works for you, at least don't let it impede on your efficiency in other areas.

- For those facing piles of paper that need to be filed, turn the piles over and begin from the bottom. That will put the oldest documents in your hands first. Assuming that you file correctly by having the most recent documents on the top of the file when you open the folder, working from the oldest documents in the piles will put them in proper order.

- The other reason that you should start from the bottom of the pile first is that much of what is in the pile may prove to be irrelevant. You may find yourself shredding many of the pages as you go, which will speed up the process.

- File by the inch. When trying to tackle large piles of paperwork, commit to filing just an inch of those piles at a time. This will keep you from being so overwhelmed by the task that you continue to procrastinate, which only allows the piles to grow larger.

- Find associated tasks that are more pleasant while you file. Listen to music that you enjoy, or sip a cup of your favorite beverage. Use those times when drop-in visitors come by who want to chat to take care of another inch of filing. You can enjoy the conversation and still be getting this essential task done.

- Open your mail by the shredder, trashcan, or recycle bin. Never lay a piece of paper down on the counter or desk without placing in a specific pile for immediate action—don't get caught in the trap of thinking you will get to it later. You probably won't, and it will end up in one of the piles that will need to be moved so you can really get back to work.

- Keep a pen/pencil and a highlighter handy when opening mail.

  o When you get something that needs to go to someone else, write their name in the upper right corner, and, if appropriate, mark the relevant section for them by drawing a highlighter line down the left of the paragraph. Lay this sheet down ONLY in either a file folder where you keep regular meeting items (such as a supervision folder) or in a folder you will empty the next time you step out of your office, delivering the paper to its proper owner immediately.

o When you get to a document that needs to be legitimately filed, mark the name of the file on the upper right corner, or highlight the file name if it appears near the top of the page. Put this in the pile to be filed, which you will do by the end of the workday.

o Act on any piece of paper that you possibly can immediately. If you can pick up the phone to answer the request for the meeting proposed in the letter, do so. If it requires an email, then respond.

o Always throw away the empty envelopes, which simply double the size of the pile if you retain them. If you really need the return address because this person isn't in your contact list, add them to your contacts now, and throw out the envelope.

- Most of us can identify junk mail from the envelope. If you know it is junk mail, throw it out (or better yet, shred it) unopened. Why waste your time getting frustrated over mail that you already know isn't of interest to you. This is a hard discipline to do, as we are so used to opening up our junk mail. Trust me, there isn't much new being mailed to you.

- When you receive magazines or professional journals, immediately look through the table of contents, select the items that may be of interest to you, and tear them out. Recycle the endless advertisements that are left. Of the articles that you tear out, staple each one together if it is multiple pages. On the upper right corner of each one (we always use this corner for consistency), date the article thirty days from the time you ripped it out. If by the time this date passes you haven't read the article, it likely isn't worth your reading. It was in a magazine, not a book, so it is likely to be about a very current topic, and will age out shortly.

- If you absolutely can't bear to tear up your magazines, either give them to your local library for an archive, or recycle them to nursing homes, hospitals, doctor's offices, schools, etc. You don't need to keep the archive yourself, and it is possible your library is already doing it. Find a new home for these treasures; get them out of your house or office. Newspapers (daily or weekly) should be bundled and recycled.

- Not all filing is done with file folders in drawers. Consider alternatives, such as loose-leaf binders, for your filing.

- When creating file folders, clearly mark the tabs in bold print with simple, concise headings. Don't overfill folders or hanging jackets, as files tend to slip behind one another and are lost to sight.

- Don't use sticky notes on the outside of file jackets for any reason. The gum on those notes is time limited, and the likelihood your note will slip off the file folder as it goes into or is pulled out of the drawer is very high. Then the sticky note simply slips to the bottom of the file drawer, and the information is lost.

- Keep often-used documents, such as reference sheets for the file or cover forms (such as for patient or client records) attached to the inside of the file folder on the left. When you open the file, this essential information will be readily available.

- Do not use paper clips to attach documents to files. See the caution above about sticky notes, as the same result applies here.

The flood of paperwork in which many of us are drowning is most likely the result of our failure to make decisions about what to do with it when we had it in our hands the first time. If you lack proper space for filing, you will need to solve that problem before you can resolve the issue of piles on your desk.

What is encouraging about this sort of problem is that it didn't occur overnight, and while it won't go away overnight either, it is solvable. It is in investment in our total effectiveness and efficiency to begin dealing with this issue at its inception. Rethink whether or not you need to print a page, whether or not you need to have copies of FYI documents, etc. Get yourself on the list that limits the amount of junk mail delivered to your door. If you are in an office, start a revolution around conserving paper by trying to create better practices and policies about printing and distributing paper documents. Not only will you discover the freedom from all those pages, but the planet will thank you, as well.

Effective E-Mailing

If you are reading this, the chances are you are a revolutionary. You have witnessed an absolute transformation in how we communicate with the introduction of the Internet, and most especially of the phenomenon of electronic mail, or e-mail. One recent study estimates that *10.1 trillion* e-mails will be sent this year worldwide. Another estimate brings that down to a more manageable number to imagine: *each day we send about 171 billion emails*. For those for whom that is still too large a number, that figures out to about *2 million e-mails sent per second*. That having been said, don't you wonder how such a disproportionate number of those end up in your computer's e-mail box?

Many believe that this revolution sent traditional letters and mail the way of parchment. When it was first introduced to the world market, it appeared that offices would soon be able to become truly paperless because digital communication was so easy. Little did we know what we had unleashed. Rather than replacing letters and communications written on paper, e-mail has more fully replaced both telephone conversations and face-to-face meetings, often with dreadful results.

Why? Why isn't e-mail an effective method of communicating, replacing our need for endless conversations with answering machines and daily games of telephone tag?

Consider this sentence: "That's not what I said." While itself seeming to be fairly innocuous and open to little interpretation, playing with the emphasis one puts on various words in the sentence can change the meaning pretty substantially. For instance, what does the sentence mean when we emphasize the first word? "**That**'s not what I said." It sounds as if we might follow that sentence with one explaining what it is we did actually say. Or what happens if we emphasize the simple word I ("That's not what **I** said") we might conclude that someone else said that, but I didn't. Or once again, if I emphasize the last word in the sentence ("That's not what I **said**.") the meaning shifts one more time, and the sentence might be taken to mean that I actually did something particular, but I said nothing about it.

This phenomenon is called tone. When we have verbal conversations with others, we pay a lot of attention the tone that they use to give us cues about what they are really trying to say. How we emphasize syllables or words, how we begin or end our sentences (i.e. whether they rise or fall at the end), our pace, our loudness—all of these qualities help define the meaning and purpose of our conversation. In truth, there are three considerations in communication, all beginning with the letter "v". There are the words we choose to use (verbal choice), how we say those words (vocal cues) and any supportive communications with our bodies—facial expressions, gestures, etc. These are visual cues. E-mail captures only the first category, which many studies say represents less than 10% of our communication power. In other words, e-mail is already 90% compromised because it cannot capture the other two categories. No wonder it is so often misunderstood!

So, what is the tone in this written sentence? If you are like many readers, you may be actually constricting your vocal chords to form the words you read, or you are listening to a voice inside your head that plays back the words you are reading so that you understand them better. The dilemma, however, is that these are your interpretations of the written words, and may or may not accurately reflect my intent in writing them. It is very difficult to capture in writing the nuances of what we are actually saying.

And this is the liability of e-mail.

Unfortunately, too few people really understand the limitations of e-mail, and so they choose to use it in place of face-to-face conversations or telephone calls. And who hasn't at some point seen an e-mail that has gone awry, either misinterpreted by its first reader, or passed along through so many other readers that ultimately someone can find something sinister in its meaning? Such stories are not mere legend in modern workplaces. As wonderful a tool as e-mail can be, it might equally be considered a hazard.

Following, then are some caveats, suggestions, and cautions about how to make e-mail serve you better.

- Use e-mail only to convey information and facts.

- Do not use e-mail to attempt to carry on personal conversations or conversations that address potentially personal issues.

- If in doubt about whether or not to put something into an e-mail, err on the side of making a telephone call, or better still, a face-to-face meeting.

- Do not type in capital letters in your e-mails. That is considered to be the equivalent of shouting, and is offensive. DON'T ARGUE ABOUT THIS! It's shouting.

- Keep your e-mail messages short and to the point. If they exceed one window or page in length, many people will delete them without reading them.

- Use concise and accurate subject lines. One rule is to use your subject line to comprise at least

50% of the content of the e-mail. The fact that so many subject lines say, "Please read" should tell us that we aren't using our subject lines effectively.

- Do not forward chain letters, jokes, pictures, etc. Especially do not forward anything that threatens either bad luck or promises blessings or good luck related to whether or not your recipient sends the message along. This isn't true just in a business situation. These messages probably shouldn't be forwarded to anyone at any time unless you personally plan to deliver on the promise that my dreams will come true if I send the message on. That could get expensive (I can dream on a pretty large scale.) Feel free to enjoy the humor yourself, and save the gag for your next cocktail party. People on your distribution list will be grateful, and you will shine as a great wit over martinis.

- If you must distribute forwards that are relevant to people from different distribution lists (meaning they may not know each other already) be sure to send them "blind carbon copy" so that people's privacy is protected. It is inappropriate simply to direct your messages with "Send All" and reveal the e-mail addresses of strangers to strangers.

- Avoid e-mail messages that simply acknowledge the receipt of the e-mail (there is an option the sender can select to know when you receive the e-mail if that is desired.)

- Avoid messages that say "O.K." or "Thank you." If either of those is an essential message, deliver it personally.

- Do not send personal messages or messages that contain inside information or jokes with the "reply all" button.

- Use the "reply all" button sparingly. Very sparingly. Only if it is essential. Almost never. Most people don't need to know what you said to the sender.

- Do not send confidential messages or information over e-mail. It is simply not confidential. Ever.

If you have sensitive information to share, do it face-to-face or by landline telephone. By the way, your cell phone isn't secure either, unless you have a very expensive scrambling system that most of us can't afford.

- When writing e-mails, structure them this way: Bullet point information first. What is the heart of this e-mail? Broader connections, friendlier conversations, or personal notes second. Details about where to get more information (links, references, etc.) last. Trust me. Those who want to know what you are writing about will not wait to the end of the e-mail. Get it to them in bullet points. Those that want every detail and piece of data will read your e-mail all the way through. Those of us who are somewhere between those two types will need to have you make kinder and gentler references in the middle.

- Use only simple fonts. Avoid ones that look like handwriting. That only clouds your clarity.

- Do not send the same e-mail twice if you can avoid it. If you so mistrust your system that you are sending it twice "to be sure it went" then you need someone to fix your computer.

- Be certain you attach any promised attachments. That is my computer's favorite mistake (I personally cannot be held responsible for it.) I cannot tell you how many times I have planned to attached one or more documents and found myself hitting the "send" button prematurely.

- Do not endlessly forward attachments from original e-mails. Once it is clear that everyone in the e-mail circle who needs to download the attachments has the chance to do so, stop forwarding them. They slow down the e-mail process and clog up mailboxes.

- Do not commit anything to e-mail that you don't mean. More than once e-mails have been used in a court of law to establish either intent or action. If you don't mean it, don't write it.

- When writing e-mails that are controversial or are emotionally charged (such as when you are angry), address the letter to yourself. Then even if you hit the button to send it, you won't regret having done so. If you decide later to send it, you can change the email address. This is safer than putting it into a draft e-box. Take some time to either personally cool off or to get a trusted friend or colleague to give you honest feedback. I strongly suggest you sleep on controversial ones (although too many e-mails can make your mattress lumpy.) Give the e-mail twenty-four hours to ripen and give yourself time enough to take a breather. As my mother used to tell me, "If it is good today, it will be good tomorrow." If you have a great point to make, it will keep. If you are right today, you can be right tomorrow instead (which will give you something to look forward to.) E-mails sent in anger or in haste have a tendency to have teeth. They will come back and bite you.

- Be very cautious about language choices in e-mails. Slang, slurs, expletives, and so forth have no place in professional e-mails. Keep in mind that what you might say in passing has a much longer shelf life if you commit it to an e-mail.

- I have a friend who follows a simple rule that I admire. If he and another person have sent back e-mails back and forth three times on one issue, he stops and picks up the phone, goes to their office, or schedules a meeting. After the third incarnation, he reasons, either they aren't going to resolve the issue without talking directly, or what they were talking about has already been lost in the body of the e-mails.

- Use capitalization and proper spelling. Use your spell-checker, for goodness sake! They don't cost you anything to use, and may save you the appearance of being an uneducated buffoon—which I know you are not. Use the shift key to create appropriate capital letters for the same reasons. And because the clearer you can be in your writing, the higher the likelihood that what you are trying to convey will actually make it onto the recipient's radar screen. And isn't that the point?

- Quote original material from other sources and credit it fully. Plagiarism in e-mails is still plagiarism.

- Avoid songs, pop-up flowers, animations, and other delightful but inappropriate add-ons. Save them for your greeting cards. And whoever invented the smiley button for e-mails is no friend of mine. Please. Greeting cards or your second-grader's math paper. Similarly, send your e-mails in plain text rather than HTML if possible. Not everyone can open up your message if dancing pixies parade in the background and music suddenly is introduced. Adding music also may make someone's otherwise quiet office become a musical hall. In an office with the door closed, that could be a nice addition. In a cube with one hundred others in earshot, that could be annoying to everyone.

- Consider turning off the pop-up that tells reminds you that you have e-mail. This can be a distraction from other tasks that require your attention. Remember, this is e-mail, and not a telephone call.

- Be very cautious about the use of colors in your typeface. Black on white is high contrast, making it easier to read. Some colors have particular meanings in cultures other than your own. They simply represent one more complication, and they aren't easier to read. Let's put it this way. Black is back.

- I really like signature blocks that include information about how to get back to the sender via telephone or fax. These can be set in most e-mail systems to be added on automatically to what you are writing. In fact, you can set up multiple signature blocks (business, personal, formal, informal, one of your many aliases) and then select the correct one for the occasion.

- Before you send huge attachments, it is courteous to inquire about the ability of the receiver to open them. Not all e-mail servers will permit gargantuan attachments, and if the system is slow, the attempts to open them will simply tie up the receiver's machine and time. Ask first.

- Avoid slogan endings. Let me give you an example. I exchanged e-mails for a while with a businesswoman for a large, well-known corporation. At the end of her emails she added the words, "Make it a fabulous day!" as part of her signature. It was interesting the first twenty times, then it became nothing but trite. And it became especially inappropriate when she railed in an e-mail about something she mistakenly thought I had done wrong, and then signed off with her traditional "Make it a fabulous day!" In a similar way, I hope you will save your religious quotes for those dear friends who may share your faith perspective or practice. Dear friends, I said. Not your business colleagues.

- Be pleasant. Despite all the other admonitions about clarity in this section, there are none that suggest you can't begin with greetings such as "Hello, _____" or even "Dear _____". Similarly, you can sign e-mails as you would a letter. Even a simple "Warm regards" may make what you have written easier to read.

- The very fact that we use acronyms such as "LOL" in our e-mails is proof enough that this medium is not a good one for personal communications. Facts and data don't require being truncated into two or three letters. We learned in the past two decades that acronyms are often a hindrance to communication in real life ("What's the ETA on the naming of the TQM team? These delays are causing a FTI, and the HH wants it PDQ or HWR." The translation: What is the expected date to name the quality management team? The delays are holding up the project, and my boss wants it soon, or there will be consequences.) They can also be a problem in our virtual communication. While many of us understand these abbreviations, others do not. This is not text messaging on your cell phone, where every letter may be costing you money. Spelling out words in e-mail simply enhances the understanding.

- Whenever possible, return e-mails within twenty-four hours. Communication follows some pretty simple rules. When people speak to you, they anticipate a nearly immediate response. When they leave you a voice mail, they want you to call back soon. They have a similar expectation of e-mails.

- Use the provider's e-mail filters to file incoming e-mails. This will allow you to send spam (e-mails that really have not meat in them) and junk e-mail to a separate folder. Then you can weed out only those you want to save and easily delete the rest. You can also set up folders to receive e-mails from selected groups, such as business groups or teams, which will allow you to focus all of your energy in one place at one time.

- Send e-mails only to those who need to know what you have written. If people are constantly looking at your e-mail and wondering, "Why was this sent to me?" your credibility is diminished. The likelihood of your next e-mail getting read goes down considerably.

- Consider answering emails only at specified times during the day. That will allow you to shut off your e-mail reminder (which has the same effect as desk stress, discussed in another section) and will permit you to chunk your activities. This means you will be doing similar activities all at the same time, keeping your brain from having to recalibrate all the time!

- Use instant messaging only when you have a single question needing a simple response. It is not a substitute for a conversation, and shouldn't be used that way. It can, however, be very effective in getting a single, simple piece of data.

- Use e-mail only in the way that you want others to use it with you. Think hard about what it is that makes a good e-mail work, and then learn from your own observations. It is a shame to have such power literally at our fingertips and misuse it as we do. Take a good tool and make it a great one!

Interruptions

Many of us plan our days well and file appropriately. The core challenge, it appears, is that even when we have done a respectable job of setting priorities and calendaring, all of our best plans get interrupted. What is probably our worst calendaring habit is that we don't plan for and allow time for those interruptions to occur, even though we can plan for them to happen as surely as we plan for our appointments.

Who hasn't had the unexpected occur? Slow traffic, illness, an unexpected telephone call, a visitor you weren't planning on, or a longer line than anticipated at the bank? Interruptions are so easily anticipated; we need to include room for them in our calendars and plans! Here are a few ideas for minimizing the impact of interruptions in your life:

- When met with the unexpected visitor at your desk or a telephone call that arrives just when you are expecting another, more important call, ask the polite but simple question, "How can I help you?" This question sets a tone for the encounter that you are in need of moving the conversation along. Often what takes time in an encounter is the perception that before a person can get to their point, they first need to create a more powerful relationship with you. That verbal dance can be time consuming! By asking this question, you are clarifying that you are ready to get down to business as soon as possible!

- When engaged in interrupting encounters summarize the conversation frequently. Use of the phrase, "What I understand you to be saying is..." Once you are on the right track, this will help bring your conversation to a clearer and more expedient close.

- If you are working in an office, turn your desk so that you are not looking out your office door. This will help avoid making eye contact with the casual person passing by, and will avoid a need for a verbal exchange.

- If you have a candy dish in your office because you like the ambiance it creates, keep in mind that such atmosphere is an open invitation for more than candy. People won't come just take your candy and walk out of your office. They will feel a need to engage you. They don't want to be seen as simply poaching your candy, even if, in fact, they are.

- If you have a chair in your office besides the one you normally sit in, you may be inviting others to come settle in for a chat. Move it out of the line of sight of the door, turn it around so the back is facing out, or fill it with items (such as you briefcase, coat, purse, etc.) to discourage unwanted occupants.

- The challenge with any interruption is getting back on task. Work on this skill whenever someone comes into your office and disturbs your workflow.

- At home, put your phone number on "Do Not Call" lists to minimize the number of telemarketing calls you receive. You can also put yourself on mail marketing lists to cut down on the unwanted mail you might get, such as credit card offers. Your registration with these services lasts only five years. It may be time for you to sign up again for these lists.

- One of the difficulties for those who work out of their home is that our homes represent challenges by their very nature. There is a load of laundry to throw in, or a well-meaning neighbor who stops by. The cat comes by and wants to be rubbed, or the dog needs to go for a walk. Invariably, the tension between the work we think we will get done and what appears because we are in our home can cut down on productivity. If possible, work in a space in your home where you can close the door. Let your family know that when the door is closed, it is as if you are at work off-site (unless, of course, a real emergency comes up, such as the house you are in is on fire!) Setting and maintaining these sorts of boundaries is extremely difficult, and will require an on-going educational process, particularly if you have younger children at home.

- Those who are fortunate enough to have office doors can close them to tell others that they need privacy or a time to concentrate. If you are in an open cube, however, that can be significantly more challenging. Try using a sign that says, "Door closed." While you can't use such a symbol every working hour of every day, you can likely use it effectively for those projects that require particular concentration. Once global company uses red baseball caps, which it issues to its employees. When someone in that company is wearing that cap, it is a clear message not to disturb them! You can also try just about anything in the door of your cubicle that will attract attention and cause people to stop. Try a small red cone such as children use in bicycle slaloms, or a beaded chain across the entrance to your cubicle. At first, you will cause a sensation, but it may be worth the extra effort it takes the first few times of explaining if it means that people learn to respect the signal.

- Schedule times when people may call you or that you will be returning calls from voice messages. Your outgoing message at either the home or the office indicates that you are in, and will be returning telephone calls at specific times, such as 11:00 and 4:00. Most people will be satisfied that you call them back, and they will wait. Be certain to honor what you promised!

- If you continue to use the pop-up message announcing that you have mail on your computer screen, shut it off. With over two million e-mails sent every second globally, there are good chances that you *do* have mail, but you really can't afford to stop what you are doing every time something pops into your in-box. Instead, check your e-mails on a regular schedule, and respond them in groups, rather than letting e-mail fill your day, keeping you from the goals that you have set.

Finding ways to avoid interruptions can be a challenging endeavor. The problem, we think, is that we can't control the behaviors of those who might come interrupt us, and we are therefore powerless to prevent them. As always, it is easier to blame others than it is to take responsibility for ourselves. In the end, however, what we get done or fail to accomplish isn't a matter of who knocks at our door, pops their head over our cubicle wall, or in some other way intrudes on our space and our day. Ultimately, we must claim the power to draw boundaries and limits. It can be a tough skill to acquire, but you can do it. And don't worry about appearing cranky to others once you start setting limits. Those interrupting co-workers will simply find some other boundary-less victim to torture with their inane questions and idle chatter. There will always be someone else who can't say, "No."

In Conclusion

If you take nothing else away from this book, I hope you will have realized in a new way (or been reminded of things you already knew) that managing yourself is the key to making the most out of your time in your day. Rather than being a victim of telephone calls, paperwork, e-mail, and interruptions, you really have the opportunity to become the master. The challenge continues to be that there are many well-meaning people and many exciting opportunities that will intrude into your plans and your day uninvited. Only you can sift and sort, and especially use that very powerful word, "No."

Not taking that sort of control can only lead to stress. Sadly, we rarely focus on what we can control, and instead see ourselves as victims of what we cannot control. When our lives feel as if they are out of control, our stress levels elevate. When our stress levels rise, our thinking clouds, and we make poorer decisions. Inevitably, that means we are entering into a vicious cycle of an increasing sense that we are out of control, which only elevates our stress again. You get the picture. Somebody has to do something, or everything swirls at an increasing rate!

The good news is that that you are that someone with the capacity to do something. It is helpful to remember, however, that if you are already swirling around over the issues described in this book, you didn't get there all at once. It was a process that got you there, and it will be a process that gets you out. Personal management skills are learnable, and they are not a single event, but they more a passage through which we must go. That process starts with a single decision to believe that we have the power to change, to reclaim our lives, and to keep our lives from overflowing in chaos. And that decision will likely emerge when we conclude that our disorganization and lack of planning has caused enough discomfort or actual pain to ourselves or those who surround us. It is out of that sense that our lives are not either as they should be or how we want them to be that we will take the necessary steps to initiate change.

One last thing—enroll others in helping you to make these changes. By getting the support of people who care about you enough to help you make adjustments to your life, you gain accountability. And frankly, there is little that is more likely to help us succeed than facing the prospect of telling someone else that we didn't have the fortitude necessary to try.